D0034529

Bicycle Stunt Riding

by Jason Glaser

Consultant:
Louis Capparelli
Bicycle Stunt Team Manager
Huffy Bicycle Company

C A P S T O N E
H I G H / L O W   B O O K S
an imprint of Capstone Press
Mankato, Minnesota

Capstone High/Low Books are published by Capstone Press
818 North Willow Street, Mankato, Minnesota 56001
http://www.capstone-press.com

Library of Congress Cataloging-in-Publication Data
  Glaser, Jason.
  Bicycle stunt riding/by Jason Glaser.
  p. cm. — (Extreme sports)
  Includes bibliographical references (p. 44) and index.
  Summary: Describes the history, equipment, and contemporary practice of
bicycle stunt riding.
  ISBN 0-7368-0167-7
  1. Bicycle motocross—Juvenile literature. 2. Stunt cycling—Juvenile
literature. [1. Bicycle motocross. 2. Stunt cycling.] I. Title. II. Series.
GV1049.3.G53 1999
796.6—dc21   98-45518
                                                                        CIP
                                                                        AC

Editorial Credits

Matt Doeden, editor; Timothy Halldin, cover designer; Sheri Gosewisch
    and Kimberly Danger, photo researchers

Photo Credits

Gene Lower, 4, 8, 18, 20, 23, 25, 28, 32, 34, 38, 40, 43
Lambert/Archive Photos, 12
Mary Messenger, 17, 31
Photophile/Matt Lindsay, 7
Photri-Microstock, cover, 14, 36
Rick Batchelder, 26
Unicorn/Aneal Vohra, 11; Jeff Greenberg, 46

Table of Contents

Chapter 1
Bicycle Stunt Riding

Bicycle stunt riders do daring tricks called stunts on BMX bikes. BMX is short for bicycle motocross. BMX bikes are small dirt bikes designed to travel over rough ground. Some people call bicycle stunt riding "BMX freestyle."

Stunt riders often practice stunts in groups. Riders teach stunts to each other. They work together to invent new stunts. They practice doing stunts on different surfaces. They may

Bicycle stunt riders do stunts on their BMX bikes.

practice on streets, sidewalks, or dirt tracks.
Riders jump or ride over obstacles such as
stairs, railings, and ledges.

Street Riding

Street stunt riding is the oldest kind of bicycle
stunt riding. Street riders practice and perform
stunts on city streets or in parks. Street riders
practice with obstacles they can find in these
places. They may slide along rails or jump
their bikes down stairs.

Unskilled or careless street riders can put
other people in danger. Many cities have
passed laws against stunt riding in public
places. Some cities have built special areas
for stunt riding and other street sports.
These sports include skateboarding and
in-line skating.

Ramp Riding

Aerial stunt riders use ramps to perform stunts
in the air. They may use ramps to jump over
obstacles. They pedal toward the ramps to

Street riders use obstacles such as stairs to do stunts.

Half-pipes are U-shaped ramps.

build up speed. Riders can jump far and high when they approach ramps at high speeds. Riders do stunts while they are in the air. They call these stunts aerials. Riders try to land their bikes safely after they complete aerials.

One popular ramp is the half-pipe. A half-pipe is a U-shaped ramp with high walls. Riders ride back and forth in a half-pipe. They build up speed by pedaling. They can perform many stunts in a row. Half-pipe riders do many aerials. Some perform stunts while their bikes are still on the ramp. The best riders can do both kinds of stunts.

Another ramp used for aerial stunt riding is the quarter-pipe. Quarter-pipe ramps have one curved side. Riders speed toward quarter-pipes to do aerial stunts.

The tops of some half-pipe walls point straight up. These half-pipes are vertical ramps. Riders call them vert ramps. Riders take their highest jumps off vert ramps.

Dirt Riding

Dirt stunt riders do stunts by riding off jumps made of mounds of dirt. Riders try to jump as high and far as they can off the mounds. Riders may combine racing with stunt riding on dirt tracks.

Some dirt riders perform aerials off dirt ramps. They do many of the same stunts ramp riders do.

Flatlanding

Flatland stunt riders do stunts on areas of flat ground, including streets and parking lots. Flatland riders perform stunts by balancing and spinning on their bikes.

One popular flatland stunt is called the bunny hop. Bunny hops are small, hopping jumps. Riders do bunny hops without using ramps or jumps. Riders lift their bikes into the air with their bodies while they are riding. They may use bunny hops to jump over small objects.

Flatland riders can perform stunts indoors or outdoors. All they need is a surface that is flat and roomy enough for them to do their stunts.

Flatland riders balance, spin, and turn on their bikes.

Chapter 2
History of Stunt Riding

The first dirt bikes had small motors. These dirt bikes were small motorcycles. People raced these bikes on dirt tracks. They called this motocross racing.

Motocross racing was very popular during the 1970s. During that time, some bicyclists rode their bicycles on motocross courses. Some of the bicycle riders built special dirt bikes for riding on the courses. The bikes had

The first dirt bikes were small motorcycles.

Bicycle motocross racers ride on dirt courses.

small, light frames and wide tires. These dirt bikes did not have motors.

The sport of riding bicycles on motocross courses became known as bicycle motocross (BMX). Riders called their dirt bikes BMX bikes for short.

Early Bicycle Stunts

BMX riders raced on motocross courses that had many mounds of dirt. Racers tried to stay on the ground when they went over the mounds. They slowed down if they went into the air. But some racers enjoyed taking long jumps. At first, they did this just for fun. They practiced performing stunts in the air. But they did not do this during races.

BMX riders soon began practicing stunts on the ground. They practiced riding on just one wheel. They practiced riding backward. Sometimes they made small jumps without holding their handlebars. Riders gathered to compare their stunts.

Stunt Riders and Skateboarders

Early bicycle stunt riders watched skateboarders. Skateboarders often did tricks on obstacles. They used many of the obstacles that street riders use today. The BMX riders learned how to do stunts on obstacles by watching skateboarders.

Some cities had special skate parks for skateboarders. Bicycle stunt riders began trying stunts at the skate parks. They tried to perform skateboard stunts using their bikes. They also invented their own stunts. The stunt riders called this freestyling. Stunt riders and skateboarders sometimes performed together in front of crowds.

Freestyling

Companies did not build early BMX bikes for stunt riding. Companies built the bikes only for racing. The bikes were not durable enough for freestyling. They broke too easily. Stunt riders had to modify their BMX bikes. These changes made the bikes more durable.

In 1983, a bicycle company called Haro built the first freestyle BMX bikes. Haro built the bikes with stronger, heavier frames than those used for racing bikes. This allowed riders to do more stunts without breaking their bikes.

Stunt bikes must be durable.

During the early 1980s, some movie studios included BMX stunt riders in movies. Riders did bike stunts for movies such as *Rad* and *E.T.* Many people liked the bicycle stunts they saw in these movies. Bicycle stunt riding became popular. Freestyle stunt riders also began appearing in commercials and on TV shows.

Early Competitions

During the early 1980s, many BMX riders performed freestyle stunts as special events at BMX races. Riders used dirt ramps and obstacles to perform stunts. Riders judged each other's stunts. But these events were not official competitions.

In 1984, BMX bike companies started holding official freestyle competitions at BMX races. Freestyle riders competed in street, ramp, dirt jump, and flatland events. Judges gave riders points based on the difficulty of their stunts. The riders with the most points won the competitions.

Riders in competitions earn points based on the difficulty of their stunts.

Chapter 3
Competition

Bicycle stunt riding competitions are popular throughout North America and Europe today. Bike manufacturers and other bike equipment companies hold stunt riding competitions year-round.

Events
Stunt riders may compete in several different events at competitions. These include street, ramp, dirt jump, and flatland events.

Riders in street competitions earn points for performing stunts on or near obstacles.

Bicycle stunt riding competitions are popular throughout North America and Europe.

Judges score street riders on a scale of one to 10. Riders earn points based on the difficulty of their stunts. They also receive points for using many different obstacles to perform their stunts.

Most ramp competitions take place on half-pipes. Riders complete as many stunts as they can in a short amount of time. They do stunts while their bikes are still on the ramp. They also do aerials. Judges rate riders on the number of stunts completed. Judges also rate the difficulty and style of the stunts.

Dirt jumpers perform aerials off dirt ramps. They usually perform only one stunt during a jump. Judges rate each jumper's stunt. Judges give points for difficulty, style, and landing. The judges announce the jumpers who have the highest scores. These jumpers each take another jump. Judges score the second jumps. They add each jumper's two scores together. The jumper with the highest total score wins.

Most ramp competitions take place in half-pipes.

Flatland riders must do a series of stunts during competition. Judges rate stunts on a scale of one to 10. Riders earn points for completing stunts. Difficult stunts are worth more points than easy stunts. Judges take away points if riders fall or make mistakes.

Team Competitions

Some stunt riding competitions feature teams. Two or more riders perform stunts together to earn points. Team members often do the same stunts at the same time.

Judges score team events the same way they score regular events. They award points for style, difficulty, and number of stunts performed. They also award points for teams that work well together. Team members must be able to time their stunts together to win team competitions.

Competitions

The biggest stunt riding competition takes place at the X-Games. The X-Games is hosted each year by a cable TV network called ESPN. Athletes at the X-Games compete in many different extreme sports. The most popular stunt riding competitions at the X-Games include vert ramp events and street events.

Team competitions feature two or more riders.

Another major stunt riding competition is at the MTV Sports and Music Festival. This competition is hosted each year by a cable TV network called MTV. Stunt bike riders and other extreme athletes compete for prizes at this competition.

Chapter 4
Equipment

The bike is the most important piece of equipment for a bicycle stunt rider. BMX freestyle bikes are different than BMX racing bikes. BMX racing bikes are built for speed. BMX freestyle bikes are built for doing stunts. Freestyle bikes must be durable. They must not break during jumps. Stunt riders choose BMX freestyle bikes that can withstand rough treatment.

The bike is the most important piece of equipment for a bicycle stunt rider.

Pegs and standing platforms provide footholds for riders during stunts.

Frames

The frame is the body of a bike. This group of metal bars holds the bike together. The seat, wheels, and handlebars all connect to the frame.

Most BMX freestyle bike frames are made of chromoly metal. Chromoly is a mix of two metals called chromium and molybdenum (muh-LIB-di-nuhm). Chromoly is heavy. Bikes with chromoly frames can weigh as much as 35 pounds (16 kilograms). Racing BMX bikes weigh only 17 to 24 pounds (8 to 11 kilograms).

Some flatland bike frames are different than other BMX bike frames. Flatland bike frames must be stronger and heavier than other BMX bike frames. This is because the stunts flatlanders perform place extra weight on the frames. Bikes with strong, heavy frames do not break as easily.

Many stunt riders sit or balance on different parts of their bikes when they do stunts. BMX freestyle frames are built so riders can move easily from part to part. Some riders attach pegs to their bike frames. The pegs provide footholds for riders during stunts. Frames must support extra weight when riders stand on pegs. Other riders attach standing platforms to their frames. Standing platforms are larger and stronger than pegs.

Rims, Tires, and Pedals

Stunt bikes must have sturdy rims. These metal rings fit inside the tires and support them. They must be able to withstand many hops and jumps. Most stunt riders use rims that are 20 inches (51 centimeters) in diameter.

Most bicycle tires have bumps and deep grooves called tread. Tires with deep tread can grip rough surfaces better than regular tires can. Most stunt riders use tires without much tread. Tread can slow down the riders.

Stunt riders spin the wheels of their bikes with pedals. The pedals pull chains connected to the back wheels. The wheels move when the chains turn. BMX racers use pedals with clips to hold their feet in place. This keeps the feet from slipping off the pedals during a race. Stunt riders do not use these clips. Clips prevent them from doing stunts that require them to take their feet off the pedals.

Tread helps tires grip surfaces.

Handlebars and Brakes

The handlebars are important in many freestyle stunts. Most bicyclists use handlebars for steering. Stunt riders use handlebars to perform stunts. They may spin their handlebars. They also may stand or sit on the handlebars.

A stunt bike has a hand brake attached to each end of the handlebar. A cable connects each brake to a wheel. One brake stops the front wheel. The other brake stops the back wheel.

Brake cables attach hand brakes to calipers. These clamps squeeze together against the wheels to slow them down. Brake cables on regular bikes can become tangled easily. Stunt bikes have special devices called gyros that prevent the cables from tangling. Gyros allow riders to spin their handlebars all the way around without tangling the cables.

Riders sit on their handlebars during some stunts.

Frame

Chain

Gear System

Pedal

Hand Brake

Handlebar

Peg

Tire Rim

Chapter 5
Safety

Bicycle stunt riding is dangerous. Riders must keep their bikes in good condition to prevent accidents. They should never try stunts with bikes that are not built for stunt riding. They must do stunts carefully so they do not hurt themselves or others.

Bodywear

The helmet is the most important piece of safety equipment for a stunt rider. Riders who do not wear helmets may suffer head injuries if they fall. Riders should wear helmets that fit

The helmet is the most important piece of safety equipment for a stunt rider.

Riders wear gloves, elbow pads, and knee pads.

well. This keeps the helmets from falling off. Many riders wear helmets with face masks.

Stunt riders also wear gloves, elbow pads, and knee pads. Riders' hands, elbows, and knees often hit the ground during falls. Gloves and pads protect riders from scrapes and broken bones.

Stunt riders should not wear loose clothing or long shoelaces. Stunt bikes do not have chain guards like most other bikes. Chain guards keep objects from becoming caught in bike chains. This can cause the chains to lock. Bikes may stop suddenly if their chains lock. This can cause riders to fall off their bikes.

Practicing Stunts

Stunt riders usually practice stunts in groups. Riders in a group can help one another if they fall.

Beginning stunt riders learn flatland stunts first. Flatland stunts are easier to do than other stunts. They also are safer because riders do not take big jumps. Most beginners do not perform stunts that involve obstacles. They usually master basic flatland stunts before trying to use obstacles.

Most beginners also avoid high jumps. They learn to control their bikes on low jumps before trying high jumps. Few beginning riders

try vert stunts. Vert stunts are the most difficult stunts to do safely. Even most experienced riders do not practice vert stunts alone.

Maintenance

Most stunt riders maintain their own equipment. They check their bikes before riding. They make sure their tires and chains are in good condition. They check all the parts to make sure nothing is loose or broken.

Stunt riders also check ramps or courses before riding. They make sure ramps are sturdy. They check for any dangerous spots on courses. By checking for safety, stunt riders can help to keep their sport safe and fun.

Vert stunts are the most difficult stunts to do safely.

Words To Know

aerial (AIR-ee-uhl)—a stunt performed in the air

bunny hop (BUHN-ee HOP)—a small bicycle jump done without the use of a ramp

calipers (KA-luh-purss)—a set of clamps at the end of a brake cable; calipers press against a wheel to stop it from turning.

chromoly (KROH-muh-lee)—a mixture of two metals called chromium and molybdenum

durable (DUR-uh-buhl)—tough and lasting for a long time

frame (FRAYM)—the body of a bike

gyro (JYE-roh)—a device that keeps brake cables from becoming tangled

maintain (mayn-TAYN)—to keep in good working condition

tread (TRED)—a series of bumps and deep grooves on a tire; tread helps tires grip surfaces.

vert ramp (VURT RAMP)—a half-pipe ramp in which the tops of the walls point straight up

To Learn More

Gutman, Bill. *BMX Racing.* Action Sports. Minneapolis: Capstone Press, 1995.

Knox, Barbara. *BMX Bicycles.* Rollin'. Mankato, Minn.: Capstone Press, 1996.

Ryan, Pat. *Extreme Skateboarding.* Extreme Sports. Mankato, Minn.: Capstone Press, 1998.

Useful Addresses

American Bicycle Association
P.O. Box 718
Chandler, AZ 85244

Canadian BMX Association
2452 Lisgar Cresent
Prince George, BC V2N 1C5
Canada

National Bicycle League
3958 Brown Park Drive, Suite D
Hilliard, OH 43026

USA Cycling
One Olympic Plaza
Colorado Springs, CO 80909-5775

Internet Sites

Canadian BMX Association
http://www.canadianbmx.org

National Bicycle League
http://www.nbl.org

USA Cycling
http://www.usacycling.org

Index